W9-DEB-407

the skinny grill cookbook

DEVELOPED BY
WILLIAMS
SONOMA
TEST KITCHEN

photographs Maren Caruso

weldon**owen**

contents

Introducing Skinny Grilling

We use this innovative, stove-top grill pan from Le Creuset® to create quick and easy recipes every day of the week. The heavy, enameled cast-iron pan features prominent ridges across the cooking surface, which deliver nicely browned marks resembling those from the rack of an outdoor grill. The Skinny Grill's high ridges elevate the food from fatty drippings so that you can manage the quantity of fat in your dishes. In addition, the slender, rectangular form of the Skinny Grill fits neatly on your stove top for maximum control of the heat. The pan's heavy-duty cast iron construction has the ability to absorb and retain heat evenly. This ensures fast and even searing, which leaves steaks, fish, chicken, vegetables, and even fruit with well caramelized exteriors.

On the pages that follow, you'll discover how to use the Skinny Grill to create a variety of delicious dishes. Grilled Rib-eye Steaks with Parsley Butter (page 33) are an easy, yet elegant main dish, while Grilled Chicken with Tropical Fruit Salsa (page 24) is a great choice for an easy weeknight dinner. Round out the plate with Grilled Succotash with Summer Vegetables & Edamame (page 40) or German-Style Potato Salad with Celery & Fresh Herbs (page 43) for a savory accent. Try Grilled Lemon Pound Cake with Macerated Strawberries (page 51) for a simple, fresh dessert. You'll find all of these and many other creative dishes, including salads, sandwiches, and more inside this book. No matter what the dish, the recipes all follow a simple formula: prep, heat, sear, and assemble, making them perfect for any time a hunger pang strikes.

Skinny Grill Features

Here are just some of the reasons why we love the Skinny Grill so much.

Durable, nonreactive surface
Requires no seasoning and needs only a thin film of oil

Versatile cookware
The pan can be used on the stove top, in the oven, or even on an outdoor grill or under the broiler

Colorful accents
The pan is pretty enough to set out on a buffet or table

Perfect size & shape
Its slender form fits neatly
on your stove top

Heavy-duty cast iron
The material retains high
heat for perfect searing

Easy to handle
Extra-wide handles are
easy to grasp, even while
wearing bulky oven mitts

Tips & Tricks

FOR USING A SKINNY GRILL

Far better than an average stove-top grill pan, the Skinny Grill has made our lives in the test kitchen—and at home—much easier. The slim size is just right for quick meals, and the grill's easy-releasing surface makes cleanup a breeze. Here are some helpful hints for using this favorite pan.

preparing to cook Before cooking, be sure to remove any labels from new cookware pieces, and then wash thoroughly (see below).

preheating To ensure good results, warm the Skinny Grill thoroughly before cooking. Plan on a few minutes to preheat the pan before placing the first ingredients on the cooking surface.

testing To test if the Skinny Grill has sufficiently preheated for cooking, look for a few slight wisps of smoke. These are a good a sign that the pan is at the right temperature to form the desired grill marks on the cooking food.

oiling To lightly oil the pan, dip a tight wad of paper towel into a small bowl of oil, allowing excess to drip off, and use a pair of tongs to run it over the pan. To protect the cooking surface, coat the Skinny Grill with a little neutral oil after washing and drying.

handling Use oven mitts when handling the Skinny Grill, as the handles can get very hot. If you are bringing the pan to the table to serve, place a trivet under the pan to protect the table from the heat and let your guests know that the pan is hot.

using The foods you can cook on the Skinny Grill are only limited to your imagination. One of our favorite things to make is a Charred Tomato Salsa. In a bowl, toss 1 jalapeño; ½ yellow onion, cut into 3 wedges; and 3 plum tomatoes with 1 tablespoon olive oil and season lightly with salt. Grill, turning, until the vegetables are nicely charred and softened, about 10 minutes. If desired, halve the jalapeño and remove the seeds. Transfer the grilled vegetables to a blender along with ¼ cup lightly packed cilantro leaves, 2 tablespoons fresh lime juice, and 1 teaspoon kosher salt. Pulse until the mixture is almost smooth, but still has some texture. Season to taste. Makes about 2 cups.

cleaning Once the pan has cooled slightly, soak it in hot soapy water. To dislodge stuck-on bits of food, scrub it with a firm-bristled nylon brush. If any residue remains even after washing, once the pan is dry, use the blunt end of a wooden skewer to scrape off any excess debris.

Fig & Prosciutto Grilled Flatbread

WITH GOAT CHEESE & ARUGULA

Delicious warm or at room temperature, flatbreads make great first courses for entertaining, or quick, but tempting weeknight meals. Here, we combine goat cheese, fig preserves, prosciutto, and arugula for the perfect mix of sweet, salty, tangy, and peppery flavors.

All-purpose flour, for dusting

1 lb prepared pizza dough, divided into 4 equal balls

Olive oil, as needed

4 oz goat cheese, crumbled

4 tablespoons fig preserves, thinned slightly with 1–2 teaspoons water

4 oz thinly sliced prosciutto

4 oz baby arugula

Juice of 1 lemon

Flaky sea salt, for sprinkling

prep On a lightly floured work surface, roll out each dough ball into an ⅛-inch thick oval, stacking the ovals between sheets of lightly floured parchment paper.

heat Warm the Skinny Grill over medium-high heat. As soon as you see a wisp or two of smoke rising from the surface, the grill is ready to use.

sear Brush one piece of rolled out dough on each side with olive oil and transfer to the grill. Cook until the dough has good grill marks and large bubbles begin to form on the top surface, about 2 minutes. Using a metal spatula, turn over the dough on the pan. Working quickly, sprinkle one-fourth of the goat cheese over the dough, then drizzle with one-fourth of the thinned fig preserves. Continue grilling until until the cheese starts to melt slightly, 1–2 minutes. Transfer to a cutting board. Repeat to grill and top the remaining three ovals of dough.

assemble Top the flatbreads with the prosciutto, dividing evenly. In a bowl, toss the arugula with the lemon juice and a small amount of olive oil. Scatter the dressed arugula evenly over the flatbreads. Sprinkle each flatbread with sea salt, cut into slices, and serve right away.

Serves 4

Grown-Up Grilled Cheese

WITH CARAMELIZED ONIONS & PEAR

Cooking a grilled cheese sandwich on the Skinny Grill creates a perfectly crisp crust with enticing grill marks. In this adult version of a childhood favorite, we stuff artisanal bread with two cheeses, caramelized onions, and slices of sweet pear.

---

4 tablespoons olive oil

1 yellow onion, thinly sliced

Kosher salt

8 slices crusty bread, such as French batard

4 teaspoons Dijon mustard

1 cup shredded fontina cheese

1 cup shredded Gruyère cheese

1 firm but ripe pear, thinly sliced

cook In a small frying pan, warm 1 tablespoon of the oil over medium heat. Add the onion and a pinch of salt and cook, stirring occasionally, until the onions are soft and caramelized, 10–15 minutes.

prep Brush one side of each bread slice with the remaining oil. On a work surface, turn 1 slice of bread oiled-side down. Spread 1 teaspoon of the mustard on the bread, then top with one-fourth of the caramelized onions, and one-fourth each of the fontina, Gruyère, and pear slices. Top with another slice of bread, oiled-side up. Repeat the assembly using the remaining ingredients.

heat Warm the Skinny Grill over medium-high heat. As soon as you see a wisp or two of smoke rising from the surface, the grill is ready to use.

sear Carefully place 2 of the sandwiches on the grill and cook until bread has good grill marks on the first side, 2–3 minutes. Using a metal spatula, flip the sandwiches over and cook until the second side has good grill marks and the cheese is melted, 2–3 minutes more. Repeat with the remaining 2 sandwiches.

assemble Cut each sandwich in half and serve right away.

Serves 4

Grilled Panzanella

WITH TOMATOES, CUCUMBER & BASIL

A traditional Tuscan salad, panzanella calls for day-old bread that is tossed with fresh tomatoes and their juices to soften and flavor it. Here, we update the classic by grilling the bread and some tomatoes for a subtle smoky flavor. Finish with your favorite extra-virgin olive oil and vinegar.

4 large heirloom tomatoes (about 2 lb total), cored and cut into wedges

½ small red onion, thinly sliced

½ cucumber, seeded and cut into ¼-inch dice

Kosher salt

4 slices country bread, each about 1 inch thick

3 tablespoons olive oil

8 oz cherry tomatoes in assorted colors

1 large garlic clove, halved lengthwise

⅓ cup loosely packed torn fresh basil leaves

Extra-virgin olive oil, for drizzling

Red wine or balsamic vinegar, for drizzling

Flaky sea salt, for finishing

prep Place the heirloom tomatoes, onion, and cucumber in a large bowl. Sprinkle with 2 teaspoons salt and toss well. Let the mixture stand at room temperature, stirring occasionally, to release the juices from the vegetables, about 30 minutes.

heat Meanwhile, warm the Skinny Grill over medium-high heat. Brush the bread slices on both sides with 2 tablespoons of the oil. As soon as you see a wisp or two of smoke rising from the surface, the grill is ready to use.

sear Working in 2 batches, place the bread on the grill and cook, turning once, until the bread has good grill marks, about 2 minutes per side. Set aside to cool. Next, toss the cherry tomatoes with the remaining 1 tablespoon oil and season lightly with salt. Arrange the cherry tomatoes on the grill and cook until lightly charred and the skins are beginning to burst, 1–2 minutes. Transfer to the bowl with the heirloom tomato mixture.

assemble When the bread slices are cool enough to handle, rub each side with the halved garlic clove. Cut the bread into 1-inch cubes and add to the bowl with the tomato mixture and accumulated juices. Add the torn basil and toss again. Drizzle with extra-virgin olive oil, red wine vinegar, and flaky salt, and serve right away.

Serves 4–6

Grilled Niçoise Salad

WITH DIJON VINAIGRETTE

This variation on the traditional Niçoise salad calls for grilling many of
the components—even the lettuce. Serve it arranged on plates or a platter,
or roughly dice the items and toss them together as a chopped salad.

3 tablespoons
Champagne vinegar

1 teaspoon Dijon mustard

1 tablespoon finely
chopped fresh tarragon

1 tablespoon finely chopped
fresh flat-leaf parsley

Kosher salt and freshly
ground pepper

4 tablespoons olive oil,
plus more for grilling

4 tablespoons canola oil

1 lb baby red potatoes, halved
and par-cooked (see page 43)

½ lb green beans, trimmed

2 hearts of romaine,
halved lengthwise

1 lb ahi tuna steak,
about 1½ inches thick,
at room temperature

½ pint cherry tomatoes, halved

4 hard-boiled eggs, halved

½ cup pitted Niçoise olives

prep In a small bowl, whisk together the vinegar, mustard,
tarragon, parsley, and 1 teaspoon salt. Slowly whisk in the
olive and canola oils to make a vinaigrette. Taste and season
with salt and pepper.

heat Warm the Skinny Grill over medium-high heat. As soon
as you see a wisp or two of smoke rising from the surface,
the grill is ready to use.

sear In a large bowl, toss the potatoes with a little olive oil,
salt, and pepper. Cook the potatoes cut-side down until they
have good grill marks, about 4 minutes. Set aside. Toss the
green beans with a little olive oil, salt, and pepper. Grill the
beans, using tongs to turn occasionally, until lightly charred
and tender-crisp, about 5 minutes total. Set aside. Drizzle the
cut sides of the romaine hearts with a little olive oil. Working
in batches if necessary, cook the romaine, cut-side down,
until slightly wilted, about 1 minute. Set aside. Drizzle the
tuna with a little olive oil and season with salt and pepper.
Cook the tuna, turning once, until it has good grill marks but
is still rare in the center, about 1 minute per side. Transfer to
a cutting board and let stand for 5 minutes.

assemble Thinly slice the tuna across the grain. Arrange
the grilled romaine on 4 individual plates. Toss the potatoes
and green beans with vinaigrette to taste and place alongside
the romaine. Arrange the tomatoes, eggs, and olives on the
plates, then add the sliced tuna. Drizzle some vinaigrette
over the top and serve right away.

Serves 4

Wedge Salad with Grilled Shrimp
& HOMEMADE THOUSAND ISLAND DRESSING

Crisp, cool iceberg lettuce and creamy Thousand Island dressing are the perfect foil for grilled shrimp in this take on a classic steakhouse-style salad. It's a great option for a casual dinner party. Use your favorite seafood seasoning blend to sprinkle on the shrimp.

½ cup mayonnaise

¼ cup ketchup

2 tablespoons finely chopped red onion

¼ cup sweet pickle relish

¼ teaspoon freshly ground pepper

Finely grated zest of 1 lemon

1 tablespoon fresh lemon juice

1 head iceberg lettuce, quartered

2 radishes, thinly sliced

1 lb jumbo shrimp (16–20 count), peeled and deveined

2 teaspoons olive oil

½ teaspoon seafood seasoning

1 tablespoon finely chopped fresh chives

prep In a bowl, whisk together the mayonnaise, ketchup, onion, pickle relish, pepper, lemon zest, and lemon juice to make a dressing; set aside. Place the lettuce quarters on individual plates and surround them with the radish slices. Place the shrimp in another bowl, add the olive oil and seafood seasoning, and toss to coat evenly. Thread the shrimp onto 4 bamboo or metal skewers.

heat Lightly oil the Skinny Grill and warm over medium-high heat. As soon as you see a wisp or two of smoke rising from the surface, the grill is ready to use.

sear Place the skewers on the grill and cook, turning once, until the shrimp are opaque and cooked through, about 3 minutes per side.

assemble Remove the shrimp from the skewers and arrange around each lettuce quarter, dividing evenly. Drizzle the lettuce with the dressing and sprinkle with the chives. Serve right away.

Serves 4

Grilled Peach Salad
WITH BURRATA & PISTACHIOS

Grilling peaches intensifies their flavors. During the summer peach season, this is one of our favorite ways to showcase their sweet, aromatic qualities. Tossed with creamy burrata cheese, fresh herbs, and crunchy nuts, this salad is light, yet hearty.

3 tablespoons white balsamic vinegar

1 teaspoon honey

¼ cup olive oil

Kosher salt and freshly ground pepper

3 fresh peaches, halved and pitted

¼ red onion, thinly sliced

4 oz mixed salad greens

¼ cup chopped fresh mint

¼ cup shelled pistachios, roughly chopped

4 oz burrata cheese, broken into bite-size pieces

prep In a bowl, whisk together the vinegar, honey, and olive oil to make a vinaigrette. Taste and season with salt and pepper. Set aside.

heat Warm the Skinny Grill over medium-high heat. As soon as you see a wisp or two of smoke rising from the surface, the grill is ready to use.

sear Arrange the peaches cut side down on the grill and cook until the peaches have good grill marks and begin to soften, 2–3 minutes. Transfer to a cutting board.

assemble If the grilled peach halves are large, cut them in half. Add the peaches, onion, salad greens, mint, pistachios, and burrata to a bowl. Add the vinaigrette and gently toss until combined. Taste and season with salt and pepper. Serve right away.

Serves 4–6

Spicy Chicken Wings

WITH SRIRACHA & LIME

Sriracha sauce adds a blast of heat to these sweet and tangy chicken wings coated with a Southeast Asian–style sauce. The sauce can be made a day in advance and rewarmed while the chicken wings cook. This recipe can be easily doubled, so it's a great dish for a game-day party.

2 tablespoons fresh lime juice

2 tablespoons honey

1 tablespoon Asian fish sauce

1 tablespoon Sriracha sauce

1 teaspoon cornstarch

2 lb chicken wings, tips removed and discarded, joints separated

1 teaspoon vegetable oil

Kosher salt

1 green onion, thinly sliced on the bias

1 lime, cut into wedges, for serving

prep In a small saucepan, combine the lime juice, honey, fish sauce, Sriracha, and cornstarch; whisk to combine. Bring the mixture to a simmer over medium-high heat, then cook until thickened, 1 minute. Transfer to a large bowl. Place the chicken wings in another bowl, drizzle with the oil, sprinkle with ½ teaspoon salt, and toss to coat.

heat Warm the Skinny Grill over medium-high heat. As soon as you see a wisp or two of smoke rising from the surface, the grill is ready to use.

sear Arrange the chicken wings on the grill and cook, turning occasionally with tongs, until the skin is crisp and meat is cooked through, 18–20 minutes total. Transfer the wings to the bowl with the sauce mixture and toss until evenly coated.

assemble Transfer the coated wings to a platter and sprinkle with the green onions. Serve with the lime wedges for squeezing.

Serves 4

Grilled Chicken

WITH TROPICAL FRUIT SALSA

Brining chicken breasts in a salt and brown sugar solution before grilling is a great way to guarantee juiciness and full flavor in just an hour. Here, we double the smoky flavor by grilling slices of tropical fruit for an easy salsa to serve atop the grilled chicken.

Kosher salt

3 cloves garlic, smashed

2 tablespoons light brown sugar

½ teaspoon cumin seeds

½ teaspoon dried oregano

¼ teaspoon chile flakes

1 cup ice water

4 boneless skinless chicken breasts, about 6 oz each, pounded until ½ inch thick

4 slices fresh pineapple, about ¼ inch thick, core removed

½ mango, peeled, pitted, and cut into slices about ¼ inch thick

Olive oil, for grilling

2 jalapeño chiles, seeded, if desired, and chopped

½ red onion, cut into ¼-inch dice

2 tablespoons fresh lime juice, plus more as desired

2 tablespoons finely chopped fresh mint

prep In a small saucepan, combine ¼ cup kosher salt, the garlic, brown sugar, cumin, oregano, chile flakes, and 1 cup tap water to make a brine. Bring to a boil over high heat, stirring until the salt is dissolved. Transfer to a heatproof bowl and stir in the ice water. Once the mixture is at room temperature, add the chicken, cover, and refrigerate for 1 hour. Remove the chicken from the brine, rinse, and pat dry.

heat Warm the Skinny Grill over medium-high heat. As soon as you see a wisp or two of smoke rising from the surface, the grill is ready to use.

sear Lightly drizzle the pineapple and mango slices with olive oil. Working in batches, cook the fruit slices until they have good grill marks and are slightly softened, 2–3 minutes per side. Transfer to a cutting board. Lightly drizzle the chicken breasts with oil and arrange on the grill. Cook, turning once, until the chicken has good grill marks and is cooked through, about 4 minutes per side. Transfer to a carving board and let rest for 5 minutes.

assemble Once the fruit is cool enough to handle, dice it and transfer to a bowl. Add the jalapeño, onion, lime juice, and mint, and mix well to make a salsa. Taste and season with salt and lime juice. Slice the chicken, arrange on plates, and top with the salsa. Serve right away.

Serves 4

Chicken Skewers

WITH YOGURT-CURRY MARINADE

Yogurt adds both a tangy and creamy quality to these chicken skewers, which are flavored with garlic, onion, and curry powder. If you like, you can substitute boneless, skinless chicken breasts for the chicken thighs, but the cooking time will be slightly shorter.

1 cup full-fat plain yogurt

2 teaspoon grated fresh ginger

1 tablespoon minced garlic

½ yellow onion, grated on the large holes of a box grater (about ¼ cup)

Kosher salt

1 tablespoon curry powder

2 tablespoons olive oil

1 tablespoon honey

3 tablespoons finely chopped fresh cilantro

1¼ lb boneless skinless chicken thighs, cut into 1-inch cubes

Steamed basmati rice, for serving

prep In a large bowl, whisk together the yogurt, ginger, garlic, onion, 1 tablespoon salt, the curry powder, oil, honey, and cilantro. Add the chicken and stir until evenly coated. Cover and marinate in the refrigerator for 1–2 hours.

heat Lightly oil the Skinny Grill and warm over medium-high heat. As soon as you see a wisp or two of smoke rising from the surface, the grill is ready to use.

sear While the grill is heating, remove the chicken pieces from the marinade and thread them relatively tightly but evenly onto 4 bamboo or metal skewers. Place the chicken skewers on the grill and cook, turning occasionally, until they have good grill marks and the chicken is cooked through, about 15 minutes.

assemble Let the chicken rest for 5 minutes. Serve the skewers on individual plates with basmati rice.

Serves 4

Glazed Pork Burgers

WITH GRILLED PINEAPPLE & RED ONION

These island-inspired burgers come together quickly for an easy weeknight supper the whole family will love. The Skinny Grill makes it easy to cook multiple elements of the same dish back to back. Round out the meal with a simple green salad or your favorite potato chips.

3 tablespoons ketchup

3 tablespoons honey

1 tablespoon soy sauce

1 tablespoon rice vinegar

1 teaspoon minced garlic

1 teaspoon finely grated fresh ginger

Pinch of cayenne pepper (optional)

1½ lb ground pork

Kosher salt and freshly ground pepper

4 slices red onion, about ¼ inch thick

4 slices fresh pineapple, about ¼ inch thick, cores removed

2 tablespoons canola oil

4 hamburger buns, split

4 Bibb lettuce leaves

prep In a small bowl, whisk together the ketchup, honey, soy sauce, vinegar, garlic, ginger, and cayenne, if using, to make a glaze. Divide the ground pork into four equal portions and shape each portion into a patty about ¾ inch thick. Season the patties lightly with salt and pepper and set aside.

heat Warm the Skinny Grill over medium-high heat. As soon as you see a wisp or two of smoke rising from the surface, the grill is ready to use.

sear Drizzle the onion and pineapple slices with oil and season with salt and pepper. Working in batches, cook the onion and pineapple, turning once, until they have good grill marks and are slightly softened, 2–3 minutes per side. Transfer to a plate. Cook the cut sides of the buns until lightly grill-marked, about 30 seconds. Set aside. Cook the patties, turning once, until they have grill marks and are slightly undercooked in the center, about 4 minutes per side. Brush the tops of each patty with the glaze, flip over, and cook for 30 seconds. Brush the patties with more glaze, flip, and cook for 30 seconds. Transfer the patties to a plate for 2 minutes.

assemble Top each bun bottom with a pork patty. Brush the patties with the remaining glaze, dividing evenly, then top with a grilled pineapple slice, onion slice, and lettuce leaf. Top with the bun tops and serve.

Serves 4

Spiced Pork Tenderloin
WITH ACORN SQUASH & TAHINI-YOGURT SAUCE

Pork tenderloin pairs beautifully with warm spices, creamy acorn squash, and a tart tahini-yogurt sauce in this dish. To save time, the squash is grilled while the pork finishes cooking in the oven. Pair this recipe with wilted greens for a well-rounded meal.

1 teaspoon ground cumin

1 teaspoon ground cinnamon

½ teaspoon ground coriander

Kosher salt and freshly ground pepper

2 pork tenderloins, about ¾ lb each

1 acorn squash, about 3 lb, halved, seeded, and cut into ½ inch slices

3 tablespoons olive oil

⅓ cup plain Greek-style yogurt

2 tablespoons tahini

3 tablespoons fresh lime juice

1 teaspoon chopped fresh cilantro

Pinch of ground cumin

2–3 tablespoons pomegranate seeds

prep In a small bowl, combine the cumin, cinnamon, coriander, 1 teaspoon salt, and ¼ teaspoon pepper and mix well to make a spice rub. Coat the pork tenderloins with the spice rub and let stand at room temperature for 30 minutes. Brush both sides of the squash slices with olive oil and sprinkle lightly with salt and pepper.

heat Preheat the oven to 350°F. Warm the Skinny Grill over medium-high heat. As soon as you see a wisp or two of smoke rising from the surface, the grill is ready to use.

sear Cook the pork on the grill, turning as needed, until browned on all sides, about 2 minutes per side. Transfer the pork to a baking sheet, place in the oven, and roast until an instant-read thermometer inserted into the center reads 145°F, about 10 minutes. Meanwhile, cook the squash slices, turning once, until they have good grill marks and are tender, 3–4 minutes on each side. Transfer the squash to a plate. Remove the pork from the oven, tent with foil, and let rest for 10 minutes.

assemble In a bowl, combine the yogurt, tahini, lime juice, cilantro, cumin, and salt and pepper to taste to make a sauce. Cut the pork crosswise into thin slices. Divide the pork among individual plates, drizzle with the sauce, and sprinkle with the pomegranate seeds. Serve with the grilled squash.

Serves 4–6

Grilled Italian Sausages

WITH ONIONS & BABY SWEET PEPPERS

Grilling a medley of colorful miniature bell peppers elevates this dish from tailgating food to a meal worthy of sitting down together. Choose your favorite fresh sausages from a butcher or meat counter at a quality market. German-Style Potato Salad (page 43) is the perfect side dish.

12 oz assorted miniature red, yellow, and orange sweet bell peppers

1 large yellow onion, cut crosswise into ½-inch rounds

1½ tablespoons olive oil

Kosher salt

⅛ teaspoon chile flakes

2 teaspoons red wine vinegar

4 links sweet Italian sausage, about 1½ lb total

prep In a large bowl, combine the bell peppers, onion, olive oil, ½ teaspoon salt, and the chile flakes. Toss well to coat.

heat Warm the Skinny Grill over medium-high heat. As soon as you see a wisp or two of smoke rising from the surface, the grill is ready to use.

sear Arrange the peppers on the grill and cook, turning occasionally with tongs, until just tender, 8–10 minutes. Transfer to a bowl. Place the onion on the grill and cook, turning occasionally, until tender, about 12 minutes. Transfer the onion to the bowl with the peppers, drizzle with the vinegar, and toss to coat. Arrange the sausages on the grill, reduce the heat to medium, and cook, turning occasionally, until the sausages are browned on all sides and cooked through, about 15 minutes.

assemble Transfer the peppers and onions to a platter. Arrange the sausages on top and serve right away.

Serves 4

Grilled Rib-Eye Steaks

WITH PARSLEY BUTTER

Rib-eye steaks are special-occasion fare, but they're so good on their own they need little adornment. For this dish, we sear the steaks, then pair them with a compound butter made with herbs, shallots, and garlic, to keep the meal easy, yet impressive.

4 tablespoons unsalted butter, at room temperature

1 tablespoon minced shallot

1 tablespoon fresh lemon juice

1 clove garlic, minced

2 tablespoons chopped fresh flat-leaf parsley

1 tablespoon chopped fresh chives

Pinch of cayenne pepper

Kosher salt and freshly ground black pepper

2 rib-eye steaks, about 1 lb each

prep In a small bowl, combine the butter, shallot, lemon juice, garlic, parsley, chives, cayenne, ½ teaspoon salt, and a pinch of black pepper. Mix well and set aside.

heat Warm the Skinny Grill over medium-high heat. As soon as you see a wisp or two of smoke rising from the surface, the grill is ready to use.

sear Sprinkle the steaks generously with salt and pepper. Place the steaks on the grill and cook, turning once, until they have good grill marks and are cooked to your liking, about 6 minutes per side for medium-rare. Transfer the steaks to a carving board and let rest for 10 minutes.

assemble Cut the steaks into slices and serve topped with the parsley butter. The butter will melt into the warm steak, creating a savory sauce.

Serves 4

Carne Asada Tacos

WITH CHARRED TOMATO SALSA

A simple marinade adds extra flavor to these grilled steak tacos. Put the steaks in the marinade in the morning, and then they're ready to grill at lunch or dinnertime. If desired, while the steak rests, warm the tortillas on the grill. Serve with Spicy Mexican-Style Corn (page 37).

3 cloves garlic

½ yellow onion, roughly chopped

½ bunch fresh cilantro, large stems trimmed

1 jalapeño chile, seeded, if desired

1 teaspoon ground cumin

1 teaspoon dried oregano

Kosher salt

Juice of 1 lime

4 tablespoons olive oil, plus more for grilling

1½ lb skirt steak, cut into 6- to 8-inch sections

Warm corn tortillas, for serving

Charred Tomato Salsa (page 10)

Accompaniments of choice: sliced avocado, crumbled queso fresco, fresh cilantro leaves, thinly sliced radishes, and/or lime wedges

prep In a blender, combine the garlic, onion, cilantro, jalapeño, cumin, oregano, 1 teaspoon salt, the lime juice, and olive oil and blend to form a smooth paste. Pour the mixture into a re-sealable plastic bag and add the steak. Seal the bag and distribute the marinade evenly around the steak. Refrigerate for at least 2 hours or up to 8 hours.

heat Oil the Skinny Grill and warm over medium-high heat. As soon as you see a wisp or two of smoke rising from the surface, the grill is ready to use.

sear Remove the steaks from the marinade, allowing any excess to drain off, and season lightly with salt. Working in batches, cook the steak pieces, turning as needed, until they have good grill marks and are cooked to your liking, about 4 minutes per side for medium-rare. Transfer the meat to a carving board and let rest for 5 minutes.

assemble Cut the steak across the grain into thin slices. Serve with warm tortillas, the salsa, and the accompaniments of your choice.

Serves 4–6

Lamb Skewer Mezze Plate

WITH GREEK SALAD & TZATZIKI

Inspired by the traditional mezze plates found in the Middle East and the Mediterranean, these lamb skewers are made with ground meat flavored with Greek spices. A cooling cucumber-yogurt sauce, a Greek-inspired salad, and grilled pita wedges round out the plate.

1 lb ground lamb

1 teaspoon ground cumin

1 teaspoon smoked paprika

¼ teaspoon ground cinnamon

Pinch of chile flakes

Kosher salt and freshly ground pepper

1 cup plain Greek-style yogurt

1 clove garlic, minced

1 English cucumber, peeled and shredded, plus ½ English cucumber, peeled and thinly sliced

2 teaspoons chopped fresh mint

3 tablespoons red wine vinegar

1 teaspoon Dijon mustard

1 teaspoon chopped fresh oregano

¼ cup olive oil

2 tomatoes, cut into wedges

¼ red onion, thinly sliced

Grilled pita wedges, for serving

prep In a large bowl, combine the ground lamb, cumin, paprika, cinnamon, chile flakes, 1 teaspoon salt, and a pinch of pepper and mix well. Divide the lamb mixture into 6 equal portions. Using your hands, affix each portion onto a bamboo or metal skewer, shaping it into a flattened log with the skewer running through the center. Refrigerate until ready to grill. In a small bowl, combine the yogurt, garlic, shredded cucumber, and mint and mix well. Taste and season with salt and pepper; set aside. In a bowl, whisk together the vinegar, mustard, oregano, and olive oil to make a vinaigrette. Taste and season with salt and pepper. Add the tomato wedges, onion, and sliced cucumber to the bowl and toss to coat with the vinaigrette.

heat Warm the Skinny Grill over medium-high heat. As soon as you see a wisp or two of smoke rising from the surface, the grill is ready to use.

sear Working in batches, cook the lamb skewers, turning once, until they have good grill marks and the lamb is cooked through, 6–8 minutes total per batch.

assemble Spoon the yogurt mixture onto a platter, then top with the lamb skewers. Arrange the tomato-cucumber salad and grilled pita wedges alongside. Serve right away.

Serves 4–6

Spicy Mexican-Style Corn

WITH CHEESE, CILANTRO & LIME

Grilled ears of sweet corn coated with cayenne-spiked mayonnaise, cotija cheese, and herbs is a simple dish often sold by street vendors in Mexico. They're easy to prepare at home using the Skinny Grill. To quickly grate the cheese, pulse small chunks in a food processor until very fine.

4 ears fresh corn

1 tablespoon canola oil

¼ cup mayonnaise

⅛ teaspoon cayenne pepper, or to taste

¼ lb finely grated cotija or crumbled feta cheese

1 tablespoon finely chopped fresh cilantro

Lime wedges, for serving

prep Remove the husks and silks from the corn and rub the ears with the oil. In a small bowl, combine the mayonnaise and cayenne pepper and mix well. On a plate, toss together the cheese and cilantro.

heat Warm the Skinny Grill over medium-high heat. As soon as you see a wisp or two of smoke rising from the surface, the grill is ready to use.

sear Arrange the corn ears on the grill and cook, rotating the ears occasionally, until the corn has good grill marks and the kernels are tender, about 10 minutes total.

assemble Lightly spread each ear of grilled corn with the mayonnaise mixture, then roll it in the cheese mixture to lightly coat. Serve the corn right away with the lime wedges for squeezing.

Serves 4

Cauliflower Steaks

WITH CAULIFLOWER TABBOULEH

This recipe is a clever way of preparing 2 whole heads of cauliflower with minimal waste. The grilled cauliflower steaks serve as a hearty meatless "steak," while the grain-free tabbouleh makes a cool, refreshing salad. A bold pesto-like mixture flavors both elements, marrying the tastes.

2 small heads cauliflower, bottoms trimmed flat

1 cup halved cherry tomatoes

¼ cup finely diced red onion

1 cup packed fresh flat-leaf parsley leaves

½ cup packed fresh mint leaves

¼ cup chopped green onion, white and green parts

½ teaspoon minced garlic

8 tablespoons olive oil, plus more for grilling

3 tablespoons fresh lemon juice

Kosher salt and freshly ground pepper

Spice mixture: 1 teaspoon each turmeric, fennel seeds, and brown mustard seeds mixed with ½ teaspoon kosher salt, and ¼ teaspoon freshly ground pepper

trim Working with the center third of one cauliflower head, cut straight down to form two 1-inch-wide "steaks." Trim the stem and leaves, leaving just enough of the stem to keep the steaks intact; transfer to a baking sheet. Trim the cauliflower that remains from the head, and place in a food processor. Repeat the process with the second cauliflower head.

prep Pulse the cauliflower in the processor until it is the size of rice grains, about 10 pulses, then transfer to a large bowl along with the tomatoes and red onion. Rinse the food processor and add the parsley, mint, green onion, garlic, 4 tablespoons of the oil, the lemon juice, 1½ teaspoons salt, and ¼ teaspoon pepper. Process until the mixture is the consistency of pesto. Transfer 2 tablespoons of the herb mixture to a small bowl and stir in 2 tablespoons oil. Stir the remaining herb mixture into the cauliflower-tomato mixture.

heat Lightly oil the Skinny Grill and warm over medium-high heat. As soon as you see a wisp or two of smoke rising from the surface, the grill is ready to use.

sear Drizzle 2 tablespoons oil onto both sides of the steaks. Sprinkle the spice mixture evenly onto both sides of the steaks. Cook the steaks, turning once, until the cauliflower has good grill marks and is tender, about 10 minutes per side.

assemble Arrange the steaks on plates and drizzle with the reserved herb oil. Serve the tabbouleh alongside.

Serves 4

Grilled Succotash

WITH SUMMER VEGETABLES & EDAMAME

This fresh summer dish is delicious served warm or at room temperature. Serve alongside grilled chicken, pork, steak, or fish, or try it over quinoa or other cooked grains for a complete vegetarian meal. Feel free to incorporate any of your favorite vegetables into the mix.

3 tablespoons sherry vinegar

1 tablespoon fresh lemon juice

2 teaspoons Dijon mustard

2 teaspoons honey

1 small shallot, finely chopped

3 tablespoons finely chopped mixed fresh herbs, such as dill, chives, mint, basil, or parsley

4 tablespoons olive oil, plus more for grilling

Kosher salt and freshly ground pepper

1 large zucchini, ends trimmed, cut lengthwise into ½-inch planks

1 large yellow crookneck squash, ends trimmed, cut lengthwise into ½-inch planks

½ bunch asparagus, trimmed

2 red bell peppers, ends trimmed, cut in half, seeded and cored

2 ears fresh corn, husks removed

¾ cup cooked shelled edamame

prep In a small bowl, whisk together the vinegar, lemon juice, mustard, honey, shallot, and herbs. Slowly whisk in the 4 tablespoons olive oil to make a vinaigrette. Taste and season with salt and pepper. Set aside.

heat Warm the Skinny Grill over medium-high heat. As soon as you see a wisp or two of smoke rising from the surface, the grill is ready to use.

sear Toss the zucchini and yellow squash with a little oil, salt, and pepper. Cook the squashes, turning once, until they have good grill marks and are just beginning to soften, about 2 minutes per side. Set aside. Toss the asparagus with a little oil, salt, and pepper. Cook, turning occasionally, until lightly charred and crisp-tender, about 3 minutes. Set aside. Drizzle the red peppers with a little oil, salt, and pepper. Cook, turning once, until lightly browned and slightly softened, about 4 minutes per side. Set aside. Drizzle the corn with a little oil, salt, and pepper. Cook, turning occasionally, until lightly charred, about 10 minutes. Set aside.

assemble Cut the grilled squashes and bell peppers into ½-inch dice. Cut the asparagus into ¼-inch pieces. Remove the corn kernels from the cobs. Combine all of the grilled vegetables in a large bowl and add the edamame. Add the vinaigrette to taste and toss to mix. Taste and season with salt and pepper and serve right away.

Serves 4

German-Style Potato Salad

WITH CELERY & FRESH HERBS

Lightly charring partially cooked potatoes gives them a hint of smokiness. The grilled potatoes are then tossed in a tart vinaigrette along with celery, onion, and fresh herbs for a zingy, fresh-tasting side dish that is refreshing change of pace from a mayonnaise-based salad.

2 lb small red potatoes, scrubbed and cut in half

4 tablespoons canola oil

2 tablespoons whole-grain mustard

2½ teaspoons brown sugar

1 tablespoon apple cider vinegar

Kosher salt and freshly ground pepper

2 celery stalks, finely diced

½ cup finely diced red onion

¼ cup chopped fresh flat-leaf parsley

2 tablespoons chopped fresh chives

cook To par-cook the potatoes, bring a large pot of salted water to a boil. Place the potatoes in the boiling water and cook until just tender when pierced with a paring knife, about 10 minutes. Drain well in a colander.

prep Transfer the warm potatoes to a bowl and toss to coat with 1 tablespoon of the oil. In a large bowl, whisk together the mustard, brown sugar, vinegar, the remaining 3 tablespoons oil, 1 teaspoon salt, and ¼ teaspoon pepper to make a vinaigrette. Set aside.

heat Warm the Skinny Grill over medium-high heat. As soon as you see a wisp or two of smoke rising from the surface, the grill is ready to use.

sear Arrange half of the potatoes on the grill, cut-side down, and cook until they have good grill marks, about 2 minutes. Turn the potatoes over and cook for 2 minutes longer. Transfer the grilled potatoes to the bowl with the vinaigrette. Repeat to grill the remaining potatoes.

assemble Toss the potatoes in the vinaigrette until evenly coated. Add the celery, onion, parsley, and chives, toss well, and serve.

Serves 6

Grilled Eggplant

WITH FETA CHEESE, PINE NUTS & SHALLOT VINAIGRETTE

Grilling eggplants imparts a smokiness that pairs perfectly with salty feta cheese and brightly flavored parsley and mint. If Japanese eggplants are unavailable, feel free to substitute 1 globe eggplant, cut in half lengthwise before slicing.

2 teaspoons finely diced shallot

2 tablespoons white wine vinegar

¼ cup plus 3 tablespoons olive oil

Kosher salt and freshly ground pepper

2 Japanese eggplants, cut crosswise into ½ inch rounds

¼ cup chopped fresh flat-leaf parsley

2 tablespoons chopped fresh mint

2 oz feta cheese, crumbled

2 tablespoons pine nuts, toasted

prep In a bowl, whisk together the shallot, vinegar, and 3 tablespoons olive oil to make a vinaigrette. Taste and season with salt and pepper. Brush the eggplant slices with the ¼ cup olive oil and season lightly with salt and pepper.

heat Warm the Skinny Grill over medium-high heat. As soon as you see a wisp or two of smoke rising from the surface, the grill is ready to use.

sear Working in batches, cook the eggplant slices, turning once, until they have good grill marks and are tender, 2–3 minutes per side.

assemble Transfer the eggplant to a platter and top with the parsley, mint, feta, and pine nuts. Drizzle the vinaigrette over the top and serve right away.

Serves 4–6

Grilled Radicchio

WITH WALNUT-HONEY VINAIGRETTE

In this stunning side dish, radicchio is paired with tart goat cheese and a sweet, nutty vinaigrette that balances the bitterness of the radicchio. You can also chop all of the ingredients and toss them like a salad to make the dish easier to serve and eat.

¼ cup walnut oil

3 tablespoons fresh lemon juice

1 tablespoon honey

Kosher salt and freshly ground pepper

2 heads radicchio

Olive oil for brushing

3 oz soft goat cheese, crumbled

½ cup walnut halves, toasted and chopped

prep In a small bowl, whisk together the walnut oil, lemon juice, honey, ½ teaspoon salt and ¼ teaspoon pepper to make a vinaigrette. Set aside. Leaving the cores intact, cut each head of radicchio lengthwise into 6 wedges. Brush the cut sides generously with olive oil, and season lightly with salt and pepper.

heat Warm the Skinny Grill over medium-high heat. As soon as you see a wisp or two of smoke rising from the surface, the grill is ready to use.

sear Arrange the radicchio wedges, cut sides down, on the grill. Cook, turning frequently, until the radicchio is browned and tender when pierced at the core with a paring knife, 4–5 minutes total.

assemble Transfer the radicchio to a platter, drizzle with the vinaigrette, and top with the goat cheese and walnuts. (Alternatively, chop the grilled radicchio and add it to a bowl along with the goat cheese, walnuts, and vinaigrette, then toss well. Taste and season with salt and pepper.) Serve right away.

Serves 4–6

Banana Boat S'Mores

WITH ALL THE TRIMMINGS

Using a Skinny Grill, the campground favorite of stuffed and topped grilled bananas can be enjoyed in the comfort of your own home. Feel free to experiment with different toppings, such as chopped nuts instead of graham cracker crumbs or peanut butter chips instead of chocolate.

4 bananas, unpeeled

¼ cup miniature marshmallows

¼ cup miniature chocolate chips

4 tablespoons crushed graham crackers

heat Warm the Skinny Grill over medium-high heat. As soon as you see a wisp or two of smoke rising from the surface, the grill is ready to use.

sear Arrange the bananas on their sides on the grill and cook, turning as needed, until the peels blacken all over, 4–5 minutes per side.

assemble Transfer the bananas to a cutting board and carefully cut a slit down the center of one side of each banana. Carefully open the bananas and divide the marshmallows and chocolate chips evenly on top. Sprinkle with the graham cracker crumbs. Place the bananas back on the grill over medium-high heat, tent with foil, and cook for an additional 30 seconds, or until the marshmallows and chocolate chips begin to melt. Serve right away.

Serves 4

Grilled Lemon Pound Cake

WITH MACERATED STRAWBERRIES

Slices of lemony pound cake are grilled and topped with strawberries for a delicious, summery dessert. The strawberries soak in a mixture of sugar and lemon juice to bring out their flavors and juices. If you're short on time, feel free to substitute purchased pound cake for homemade.

4 cups fresh strawberries, hulled and quartered

1 tablespoon sugar

1 tablespoon fresh lemon juice

Lemon Pound Cake (page 52), cooled

Crème fraîche, whipped cream, or vanilla ice cream, for serving

prep In a bowl, combine the strawberries, sugar, and lemon juice and toss well. Let the strawberries macerate for at least 20 minutes. Cut the pound cake crosswise into 6–8 slices.

heat Warm the Skinny Grill over medium heat. As soon as you see a wisp or two of smoke rising from the surface, the grill is ready to use.

sear Working in batches, place the cake slices on the grill and cook, turning once, until the slices have good grill marks, about 1½ minutes per side, watching carefully so that they do not burn.

assemble Arrange the cake slices on individual plates. Spoon the strawberries with their juices over the top. Accompany with crème fraîche and serve right away.

Serves 6–8

Lemon Pound Cake

Slices of this tender, lemon-scented pound cake gain a slightly smoky flavor when cooked on a Skinny Grill. The cake is easy to make, requiring only one bowl and just over 1 hour of baking time. Use this to make the Grilled Lemon Pound Cake with Macerated Strawberries on page 51.

Vegetable shortening, for greasing

All-purpose flour, for dusting

1½ cups plus 2 tablespoons cake flour

⅛ teaspoon baking soda

⅛ teaspoon table salt

9 tablespoons unsalted butter, at room temperature

4 oz cream cheese, at room temperature

1½ cups sugar

3 large eggs

1 teaspoon vanilla extract

2 tablespoons fresh lemon juice

Finely grated zest of 1 lemon

prep Position a rack in the lower third of the oven and preheat to 325°F. Grease and flour a 8½-by-4½-inch loaf pan; tap out the excess flour.

mix Over a sheet of parchment paper, sift together the cake flour, baking soda, and salt; set aside. In the bowl of a stand mixer fitted with the paddle attachment, beat the butter and cream cheese on medium speed until creamy and smooth, about 30 seconds. Gradually add the sugar and beat until light and fluffy, about 5 minutes, stopping occasionally to scrape down the sides of the bowl. Increase the speed to medium-high and add the eggs one at a time, beating well after each addition. Beat in the vanilla and lemon juice. Reduce the speed to low and add the flour mixture in 3 additions, beating each addition until just incorporated and stopping occasionally to scrape down the sides of the bowl. Using a rubber spatula, fold in the lemon zest.

bake Spoon the batter into the prepared pan. Bake until the cake is golden and a toothpick inserted into the center comes out clean, 70–75 minutes. Transfer the pan to a wire rack and let the cake cool upright in the pan for 15 minutes. Remove the cake from the pan and let cool completely.

Makes 1 loaf

index